17
24

Also by Guy A. Zona

The House of the Heart Is Never Full

The Soul Would Have No Rainbow If the Eyes Had No Tears

Eyes That See Do Not Grow Old

Even Withered Trees Give Prosperity to the Mountain

If You Have Two Loaves of Bread, Sell One and Buy a Lily

True Love Is Friendship Set on Fire

And Other Proverbs of Love

Guy A. Zona

A TOUCHSTONE BOOK
Published by Simon & Schuster

TOUCHSTONE
Rockefeller Center
1230 Avenue of the Americas
New York, NY 10020

TOUCHSTONE and colophon are registered trademarks of Simon & Schuster Inc.

Designed by Judy Wong

Manufactured in the United States of America

1 3 5 7 9 10 8 6 4 2

Library of Congress Cataloging-in-Publication Data
True love is friendship set on fire : and other proverbs of love / [compiled by]
Guy A. Zona.
p.   cm.
"A Touchstone book."
1. Proverbs.   2. Quotations.
3. Love—Quotations, maxims, etc.   I. Zona, Guy A.
PN6525.L68T78   1998
302.3—dc21   97-33354
CIP
ISBN 0-684-83492-8 (alk. paper)

This book is dedicated to my five children with humble and acceptable pride, Nicholas, Beverly, Guy, Dean, and Earl, each of whom has been my instructor in the art of loving. The grandchildren they have presented me with, Rina, Nicolette, Bethany, Jordan, Matthew, Victoria, and Kelsi, have taught me an infinitely deeper and more meaningful form of love as well as the true meaning of immortality. As a father and grandfather, I could not be more proud or pleasantly pleased than to dedicate a book about love to those I love the most, unconditionally and unceasingly. I love you all my pretty ones.

Introduction

Having this work published is the realization and fulfillment of a lifelong dream. In doing the enormous amount of research required to amass such a fine collection of the proverbs of love from countries spread throughout the globe, I kept on telling myself that it was a true labor of love. Upon reflection, I realized that while that word's true and complete definition somewhat escapes us, we are all familiar with the mystique, power, and rewards of "love." It is a word we all use, a word we are all quite certain we understand, yet one will find countless volumes written on the subject in valiant attempts to explain it. There are innumerable poems and songs that appropriately have love as their themes, and love is one of the first words we are taught as children.

In an effort to better understand the very word, I looked up "love" in my massive dictionary. I then consulted my always reliable thesaurus. I was immediately amazed but pleasantly pleased that there are well over one hundred different words (from "ardent" to "zeal") to describe, identify, and otherwise explain that one word. It is no wonder then, nor is it any spectacular revelation, that love is the most sought-after endeavor, most desired accomplishment, and most longed-for treasure of all human emotions. Quite simply, we all need and want to love and be loved.

In this collection, one will find proverbs from all over the world that pleasantly deal with the enchantment of love, its durability, virtues, and, yes, its powers.

Because love by its very nature seeks union, and the traditional and historical display of this union is marriage, there are several very well-worded marriage proverbs. Some of my favorites are:

Who marries might be sorry; who does not marry will be sorry.
Marriage is a game best played by two winners.
Love is a flower which turns into fruit at marriage.

Associated very closely with the union of marriage there are other bonds of togetherness and our need for togetherness, which are delicately displayed in such proverbs as:

To one dove alone cherries are bitter.
Part your tents, bring your hearts together.

The glory, omnipotence, and magnitude of love is beautifully stated as:

Man has one beauty, woman a hundred,
jewels a thousand, and love a million.

Among the many facets of love is its inherent durability and permanence as stated in the following proverbs:

Highways can be worn out, but
not love and attachment.
Love views life from the point of view of eternity.

And hence, in the following pages we run the gamut from the unselfish, non-demanding, non-sexual brotherly love of agape to desirous Eros love and back once again to the love that seeks the union between two people. In closing, let me quote one of my favorite proverbs, which originated with Confucius:

> *Immature love says: "I love you because I need you."*
> *Mature love says: "I need you because I love you."*

And it will do us all well to remember that:

> *"A love that can last forever takes only a second*
> *to come about."*

—Guy A. Zona

Of time, love, and thought, the heart is full.
(Africa)

Distance lends enchantment to love.
(Korea)

A loving heart is a child; it hopes what it wishes.
(Germany)

When the heart is in love, beauty is of no account.
(Afghanistan)

Love is something that you can leave behind you when you die. It's that powerful.
(Native American)

He who loves the vase, loves also what is inside.
(Zanzibar)

Do not love a woman because she is young, nor
cast her off because she is old.
(Russia)

A loving heart spins much flax.
(Romania)

The one we love is always beautiful.
(Norway)

The heart that loves is the beginning of benevolence.
(Japan)

Not with your kindred, but with whom you love.
(Mexico)

Love teaches asses to dance.
(France)

Love overlooks defects, and hatred magnifies shortcomings.
(Lebanon)

Loving one who does not love you is loving the rain that falls
in the forest.
(Kenya)

True love comes after marriage.
(Jamaica)

Through wisdom a house is built, and by love it prospers.
(Finland)

Though you be two that love, let there be one heart
between you.
(Italy)

Who exposes himself to love, exposes himself to suffering.
(Chile)

✗ Tell me whom you love and I'll tell you who you are.
(Portugal)

✗ Don't let your heart lean on riches but on love.
(Malagasy Republic)

✗   The heart of one void of love is harder than iron.
(India)

Better to love me little, but love me long.
(Yiddish proverb)

✗   A loving heart is not only the greatest virtue but the parent
of all other virtues.
(China)

The thoughts of his heart, these are the wealth of a man.
(Burma)

✗   A heart without love is a violin without strings.
(United States)

*T*o one dove alone cherries are bitter.
(Hebrew proverb)

*M*other love is the cream of love.
(Greece)

X *I*t is better to love than to be loved.
(Estonia)

*L*et the love that will not glow, slumber.
(Wales)

*H*ighways can be worn out, but not love and attachment.
(Vietnam)

Handle with care: women, glass, and love.
(Sweden)

If you would live long, open your heart to love.
(Bulgaria)

Love understands love, it needs no talk.
(Japan)

The disease of love has no physician.
(Zanzibar)

Faith dares everything and love bears everything.
(Jamaica)

✖ Who marries might be sorry; who does not marry
will be sorry.
(Bohemia)

Love and brandy have soothing aftereffects.
(Mexico)

The love of one's wife is religion.
(Lebanon)

If any man wishes to escape idleness, let him fall in love.
(Ancient Rome)

✗ The heart that loves is always young.
(Hebrew proverb)

Let your love be like misty rain: little in coming but flooding the river.
(Malagasy Republic)

There was never a fair prison, nor a love with a foul face.
(England)

Excesses are rare when love is in one's heart.
(Australia)

Kisses are the language of love.
(Greece)

Marrying for love is risky, but God smiles on it.
(United States)

                                  Mother love is always renewed.

(France)

Love is caught with a silken thread, but driven away
with a ship's cable.

(Estonia)

Love blinds itself to all shortcomings.

(Lebanon)

Love laughs at locksmiths.

(England)

Love cannot dwell with suspicion.

(Denmark)

Rare and far-between visits increase love.
(China)

You don't trouble to look at the good plate of meat before
you, but the face you love you look at always.
(Australia)

In a beloved wife there is no evil.
(Africa)

If love thinks no evil, we may be sure that it speaks none.
(Chile)

Marriage is a game best played by two winners.
(United States)

A love that can last forever takes only a second
to come about.

(Cuba)

*W*here the heart is willing to love it will find a thousand ways,
but where it is unwilling, it will find a thousand excuses.

(Borneo)

*F*ind as much love as was given by thy father and
mother many times.

(Italy)

*I*f there is love in your heart, your home is like a palace.

(Canada)

House and wealth are inherited from our fathers; but
a sensible wife is a gift from the Lord.
(Proverbs 19:14)

They wooed her and she resisted; they neglected her and she
fell in love.
(Middle East)

Sooner may you stop the sea's mouth with wax than stifle the
prayer which proceeds out of a heart in love.
(Afghanistan)

✗   Love makes obedience light.
(Australia)

Where love is the seasoning, the dish will please
anyone's palate.
(Ancient Rome)

Our loving is always the dupe of the heart.
(France)

Where the ache, there the hands; where the eye,
there the love.
(Finland)

Love is like fog, there is no mountain on which
it does not rest.
(Yiddish proverb)

Love is the perfect of the verb "live."
(Ireland)

If you love your love, you should love her thoughts, too.
(India)

The remedy for love is land to separate it.
(Mexico)

Don't love me as you do a door to be pushed to and fro.
(Malagasy Republic)

In dreams and in love nothing is impossible.
(Hungary)

Even if it were to rain gold a lover would never become rich.
(Holland)

To be loved, be worthy of love.
(Hebrew proverb)

Cold is the love that is put out by one blast of wind.
(Wales)

The lover who suffers not anguish knows not
the worth of pleasure.
(Turkey)

A life without love is as bleak as a year without summertime.
(Sweden)

Choose your love, then love your choice.
(China)

Love is like trees in a farm, they lean toward each other.
(Sudan)

Where there is love, there is no sin.
(Spain)

Love is sweet captivity.
(Slovakia)

Love that blushes is a flower; love that pales is a tragedy
of the heart.
(Poland)

True love shows itself in time of need.
(Scotland)

It is not the gift that is precious, it is the love.
(Russia)

Marriage is the supreme blunder that all people wish to make.
(United States)

True love can endure no concealment.
(Spain)

Love is a flower which turns into fruit at marriage.
(Finland)

Reason on love and you will lose your reason.
(France)

Hearts communicate with each other when love abounds.
(Russia)

Where there is love there is also a quarrel.
(Romania)

Everything will perish except love and music.
(Ireland)

Superficial love is like smoke; it quickly dissipates.
(Philippines)

The heart is a dry pod, it will bear only one love.
(Norway)

Love is like seaweed; even if you have pushed it away, you will not prevent its coming back.
(Nigeria)

Love and show; hate and hide.
(Morocco)

Love without tribulations becomes stale.
(Italy)

An amorous visitor finds a thousand miles but one.
(Japan)

Don't wait for slander to enter into your ears, lest it turn former love into hatred.

(Korea)

Mutual love is often better than natural brotherhood.

(Sudan)

Lovers ever run before the clock.

(England)

I love the man as a standing tree.

(Jamaica)

Love rules its kingdom without a sword.

(Italy)

The first sigh of love is the last sigh of wisdom.
(France)

What is in your heart concerning thy love is in his heart
concerning you.
(Hebrew proverb)

Love lives in cottages as well as in castles.
(England)

Part your tents, bring your hearts together.
(Egypt)

Mistrust is an ax at the tree of love.
(Russia)

Love cures the very wound it makes.
(Greece)

Love makes cottages manors, and straw into silken ribbons.
(Estonia)

Love teaches eloquence.
(England)

Labor is light where love is the wages.
(Ireland)

Love is like the smallpox; it comes in the natural way
and can't be prevented.
(United States)

   Anger beats the shoulders with its own rod until they bleed;
love tints the face with its own rouge.

(Finland)

Love prefers the middle path.

(Denmark)

When passionately in love, one becomes stupid.

(Japan)

Where love reigns, the impossible may be attained.

(India)

There are a thousand miseries in one falling in love.

(China)

Love speaks, even when the lips are closed.
(Germany)

Love cannot live in solitude; neighbors are sure
to grow up around it.
(Korea)

Love without return is like a question without an answer.
(Germany)

As is the lover, so is the beloved.
(Italy)

Where distrust enters, love is no more than a boy.
(Chile)

A blow from our lover is as sweet as the eating of raisins.
(Egypt)

*S*low are the steps of those who leave their love behind.
(England)

*T*he hardest job a child faces is that of learning love
without seeing any.
(India)

*F*irst love, last love, best love.
(Canada)

*I*t is not good that man should be alone.
(Genesis 2:18)

A man is often too young to marry but a man is never too old to love.
(Finland)

Love's greatest miracle is the curing of coquetry.
(Mexico)

Love is the fulfilling of the law.
(Romans 13:8)

Sometimes love has been planted by one glance alone.
(Middle East)

There are no herbs for curing love.
(Ancient Rome)

The soul is not where it lives, but where it loves.
(England)

A wife is like a blanket; when you cover yourself with it, it
irritates you; yet if you cast it aside, you feel cold.
(Africa)

It is astonishing how little one feels poverty when one loves.
(Ireland)

They who want to love must love.
(United States)

The greatest thoughts are from a loving heart.
(France)

Love looks through spectacles that make copper appear gold; poverty like riches; and tears like pearls.
(Peru)

Love enters even though it is forbidden.
(Africa)

Those in love always know the time.
(Germany)

He who truly loves never forgets.
(Mexico)

You can't love God without loving man.
(Yiddish proverb)

The man who has never made a fool of himself in love
will never be wise in love.
(Bulgaria)

Live in my heart and pay no rent.
(Ireland)

From the one you love most you often suffer the most.
(Slovakia)

None love except those who wish to love.
(Wales)

Love is the companion of blindness.
(Middle East)

Love is strong as death, jealousy is cruel as the grave.
(Solomon 8:6)

Love and foolishness differ from each other only in name.
(Hungary)

My true love is the only person with whom I may be sincere.
In her presence I may think aloud.
(United States)

Love grows best with obstacles in its way.
(Germany)

To love mankind is easy; to love man is difficult.
(Hebrew proverb)

Love can neither be bought nor sold; its only price is love.
(United States)

The loss of love is a terrible thing; they lie who say that
death is worse.
(Poland)

To love a thing means wanting it to live.
(Confucianism)

Love and blindness are twin sisters.
(Russia)

Friendship confides the secret, love divulges it.
(Hebrew proverb)

There is more pleasure in loving than in being loved.
(England)

A tongue is not necessary to declare love.
(Wales)

One cannot be a lover by force.
(Turkey)

Love is a deep well: A man may drink from it often, but he
falls into it only once.
(Sweden)

Love is like a caravan where one only finds what one brings.
(China)

The way to the loved one is never thorny.
(Sudan)

True love is like ghosts, which everybody talks about and few have seen.
(Egypt)

Often he who afflicts, loves.
(Holland)

Love will creep where it cannot run.
(England)

Love is a ring and a ring has no end.
(Russia)

Love is never lost. If not reciprocated it will flow back to
soften and purify the heart.
(Greece)

✗ *I* went in search of love and lost myself.
(India)

Love is never without some thorns.
(Slovakia)

We are shaped and fashioned by what we love.
(Germany)

✗ *It* is the people, not marriage, that fail.
(United States)

Pleasures of love last but a moment; pains of love
last a lifetime.
(France)

Love reckons hours for months, and days for years, and
every little absence is an age.
(Canada)

Love knows not labor.
(Italy)

Hearts are the depositories of secrets, lips their locks, and
tongues their keys.
(Middle East)

Things never change since the time of the gods, the flowing of
water, the way of love.
(Japan)

Who finds not love finds nothing.
(Puerto Rico)

Absence is the enemy of love, as the distance is from the eyes,
so it is from the heart.
(Dominican Republic)

If you love, you are the slave; if you are loved, you are
the master.
(Poland)

Ranking the effort above the prize is called love.
(Korea)

Who loves much, fears much.
(Spain)

Expel avidity from your heart; the fetters will be loosened
from your feet.
(Egypt)

Love and light cannot be hidden.
(Scotland)

In love, as in war, each man must gain his own victories.
(United States)

Love gives wit to fools, but it often takes wit away
from wise men.
(Wales)

True love is friendship set on fire.
(France)

Short love brings a long sigh.
(Romania)

All true love is grounded in respect.
(Japan)

Thirst is the end of drinking; sorrow, the end of love.
(Ireland)

Love has no language to be heard by the ears, only felt
in the heart.
(England)

Love is a thing most plentiful, both in honey and in gall.
(Ancient Rome)

Let nothing on earth sadden you so long as you can still love.
(Hungary)

In love the one first cured is the most completely cured.
(France)

Love is an excuse for its own faults.
(Italy)

Love is the salt of life.
(Philippines)

One does not love if one does not accept.
(Nigeria)

In love's wars, he who flees is the conqueror.
(Holland)

Ignorance and bungling with love are better than wisdom and
skill without it.
(Ireland)

Two loves will not stay together in one heart.
(Morocco)

Love is more precious than all other treasures.
(Japan)

Love is the prevailing breeze in the land of youth.
(Italy)

Love is that condition in which the happiness of another person is essential to your own.
(Chile)

The boat of affection ascends even steep mountains.
(India)

Love is nature's second sun.
(Holland)

The eye of the needle does not accept two threads; the hearts of people cannot contain two loves.
(Sudan)

Love requires faith and faith requires affirmation.
(Italy)

Love, pregnancy, and riding a horse cannot be hidden.
(Vietnam)

The only unpardonable sin is the murder of love.
(Scotland)

Who loves talks of it often.
(Egypt)

Love covereth a multitude of sins. It forgives and forgets and therein it proves itself to be of God.

(1 Peter 4:8)

The heart and the tongue are small, but they show the greatness of the man.

(Germany)

The sources of beauty and satisfaction may be found close at hand within the range of one's own ability to love.

(Australia)

Do not belittle the wife, she is the home.

(Africa)

Love is the mother of all godliness.
(United States)

A man who plants trees loves others besides himself.
(England)

Love your wife as you love yourself, but honor her more.
(Jewish proverb)

If love be timid, it is not true.
(Spain)

You can tell lovers from their faces.
(Africa)

❦ *I* have tasted earthly happiness; I have lived and I have loved.
(Germany)

❦ *We* can see a rose, but not its perfume; we can feel love, but
it cannot be seen.
(Lebanon)

❦ *People* in love imagine dreams of their own.
(Ancient Rome)

A loving heart will often sigh.
(France)

❦ *Love* and prudence are absolutely incompatible.
(Bolivia)

Love flies away and the pain remains.
(Cuba)

Love is all we have, the only way that each can help the other.
(Finland)

Three that come unsought: fear, jealousy, and love.
(Ireland)

One hour for your love, one hour for your God.
(Middle East)

There is no harvest for the heart, the seeds of love must be
eternally resown.
(Malagasy Republic)

There is no fear in love, but perfect love casts out fear.
(1 John 4: 18)

Love knows hidden paths.
(Germany)

Next to love, quietness.
(United States)

Love and eggs should be fresh to be enjoyed.
(Russia)

Prayer is not an option. Neither is love.
(Hebrew proverb)

Though love is blind, yet it is not for want of eyes.
(England)

He who loves is remembered by all.
(Wales)

Let him not be a lover who has not courage.
(Italy)

In love, to submit is to be victorious.
(Japan)

Forced love does not last.
(Holland)

The lover walks in the snow and does not make his
tracks visible.

(Turkey)

Love is the joy of the good, the wonder of the wise, and the
amazement of the gods.

(Italy)

When the quarrels are many, deep becomes the love.

(Sweden)

Man has one beauty, woman a hundred, jewels a thousand,
and love a million.

(India)

Between a man and his wife nothing ought to rule but love.
Authority is for children and servants.
(United States)

Love is liberal.
(England)

Love me as you do cotton: Add to the thin and rejoin
the broken.
(Morocco)

Love is like the eye of a needle: without it, there would be
no mending.
(Spain)

A secret love is always a true love.
(Slovakia)

Who loves well sees from afar.
(Colombia)

Where there is much love, there is seldom great boldness.
(Spain)

Where there is much love, there is much mistake.
(England)

Love is the water of life and lust is the lure of death.
(Russia)

It is a beautiful necessity of our nature to love.
(Nigeria)

Love has never been very strong if it turns for a trifle.
(Scotland)

A man is only the head, a good wife is the crown.
(Proverbs 12:4)

Faith makes all things possible and love makes all things easy.
(United States)

Love is a tickling sensation around the heart.
(Wales)

Who would give a law to lovers? Love is unto itself
a higher law.
(Hebrew proverb)

Blind love mistakes a harelip for a dimple.
(France)

Love hides ugliness.
(Ireland)

Love is a credulous thing.
(Ancient Rome)

War is the law of violence; peace is the law of love.
(Japan)

Of soup and love, the first is best.
(England)

Who loves most, rebukes most.
(France)

It is not decided that women love more than men, but it is
indisputable that they love better.
(Australia)

Who loves, believes.
(Italy)

True love is sweet until the end.
(Philippines)

Sudden love is divided between the days.
(Morocco)

Love as the cotton does, which in life shields you and goes with you in death.
(India)

He who loves has every pocket filled with hope.
(Germany)

The greatness of love obliterates conventions.
(Sudan)

Love is like tears: it is born in the eyes and falls on the breast.
(Italy)

The man who is not jealous in love, loves not.
(Egypt)

Wedlock is like a besieged fortress; those who are outside wish
to get in, and those who are inside wish to get out.
(Middle East)

Love is more afraid of change than destruction.
(Germany)

Lovers live by love as larks live by leeks.
(Wales)

One flower alone makes no garland.
(Yiddish proverb)

Love is like a sprain; a second time it arrives more easily.
(Spain)

When the fire of love is extinguished, one finds cinders
but not gold.
(Poland)

A lover is unmindful of any charcoal on the body.
(Africa)

Love sought out is good, but love discovered is superior.
(Austria)

Love letters need not be dated.
(Germany)

Two who never believe the report of your death: the person
who hates you and the person who loves you.
(Ireland)

Music is nothing if love is gone.
(Middle East)

Many waters cannot quench love, neither can floods drown it.
(Song of Songs 8:7)

In love and war no time should be lost.
(United States)

In the eyes of the jealous, a mushroom grows into a palm tree.
(Nigeria)

Love tells us things that are not always accurate.
(Russia)

Love without rebuke is no love.
(Hebrew proverb)

In love there is no lack.
(England)

✗ The supreme happiness of life is the conviction
that we are loved.
(Denmark)

It is easy to reconcile where there is love.
(Wales)

Woe to they who love and are not loved.
(Scotland)

The rope has never been made that binds love.
(Sweden)

The lover loves not at all who knows not when
to make an end.
(Holland)

Love is full of busy fear.
(England)

Love is the lodestone of life.
(Australia)

He whom we love is white even when unwashed.
(Russia)

Who are loved in this world are loved in heaven.
(India)

Where there is great love, there is great pain.
(Italy)

Love is a perfume that you cannot pour on others without
spilling a little on yourself.
(United States)

Who loves ugly things thinks them beautiful.
(Spain)

May the sun set for me where I keep my love.
(Belgium)

He loves me for little who hates me for naught.
(Scotland)

Love makes time pass away, and time makes love pass.
(Switzerland)

Blossoms are scattered by the wind and the wind cares nothing, but the blossoms of the heart no wind can touch.
(Korea)

Strong love is not soon forgotten.
(England)

True lovers are shy when people are by.
(Australia)

Whom we love the best, to them we say least.
(Wales)

Lovers always think that other people have had their
eyes put out.
(Spain)

Our perfection stems from our ability to love.
(Italy)

Love with loyalty.
(France)

There is always some madness in love. But there is also always some reason in madness.
(Germany)

If love interferes with your business, quit your business.
(Ireland)

The soul is more where it loves than where it lives.
(Ancient Rome)

Love yields to caresses, not to compulsions.
(Hebrew proverb)

If we cannot have what we love, we must love what we have.
(Norway)

The more one loves the other, the less one knows the other.
(Italy)

Love unexpressed is useless.
(Philippines)

The loves of youth are as a cluster of silver buds, but
the love of maturity is like unto golden flowers.
(Japan)

If given with love, a handful is sufficient.
(India)

Love has taught mankind to reason.
(Middle East)

Love is like soup: The first mouthful is very hot and the ones
that follow become gradually cooler.
(Australia)

Lovers measure time with desire.
(Germany)

Unrequited love is like a question without an answer.
(Poland)

Love is above king or kaiser, lord or laws.
(England)

Love is a sweet torment.
(Wales)

In love and in death, it is of no avail to be strong.
(Spain)

That which is loved by the heart is a remedy.
(Africa)

Love knows neither winter nor summer.
(Switzerland)

Where the first love is written, time does not cancel
a single line.
(Germany)

If love is a sickness, patience is the remedy.
(Nigeria)

Nothing more excites all that is noble than virtuous love.
(Greece)

Love is not blind, it merely doesn't see.
(Austria)

Love can make any place agreeable.
(United States)

No joy emanates from a person without love.
(Russia)

Where there is love, there is God; where there is God,
there is love.
(Finland)

Love is called the daughter of the skies because it grows wings quickly.
(Hebrew proverb)

All is fair in love and war.
(England)

Who loves me not, let him not rebuke me.
(Wales)

Love or fire in your trousers is not easy to conceal.
(Sweden)

To love and be wise is impossible.
(Spain)

He who is dear to me is dear even in his commission
of a fault.
(India)

Love makes a good eye squint.
(England)

He that has love in his breast has spurs in his sides.
(Australia)

Lovers, like bees, spend a honeyed life.
(Italy)

Love isn't love until you give it away.
(United States)

It is easy to persuade one who is loved.
(Wales)

Who loves truly, forgets slowly.
(Spain)

He who loves without being loved is charmed with love.
(France)

There is no pain like that of refusal.
(Ireland)

Whatever makes an impression on the heart seems lovely
in the eye.
(Portugal)

Hot love, hasty vengeance.
(Scotland)

The momont one is in love, one becomes quite amiable.
(France)

The falling out of lovers is the renewing of love.
(Italy)

Love reaches even to a crow on a roof.
(Japan)

Let your love be as a Hindu wife; with you in life and with you in death.
(India)

In hunting and in lovemaking, one knows where one begins,
but not where one ends.
(Germany)

Love, knavery, and necessity make men good orators.
(England)

Follow love and it will flee; flee love and it will follow you.
(Austria)

Love in prosperity as well as in adversity.
(Africa)

Everything disturbs an absent lover.
(Spain)

Absence is to love what air is to fire—it puts out a little one and fans a big one.
(Spain)

Love does not choose the blade of grass on which it falls.
(Africa)

We never love a person, but only their qualities.
(Kenya)

Love views life from the point of view of eternity.
(Greece)

Love looks for love again.
(Finland)

Not what is beautiful is loved; rather what is loved
is beautiful.
(Germany)

Three counselors not to be trusted: wine, night, and love.
(Austria)

Love lightens labor and sweetens sorrow.
(Hebrew proverb)

No one can live on love, but they can die for it.
(Sweden)

Where there is love, impossibilities will become possible.
(India)

He who forces love where none is found
Remains a fool the whole year round.
(Germany)

Love spread on bread is a long way from bread and butter.
(Egypt)

Love is strongest in pursuit; friendship in possession.
(United States)

The anger of those in love is like the spider's web.
(Italy)

One always returns to one's first love.
(Africa)

He who loves well, obeys well.
(Spain)

Love conceals ugliness, but hate sees all of the faults.
(Ireland)

Love and knowledge live not together.
(Wales)

Love levels all inequalities.
(Italy)

Love is beyond one's consideration.
(Japan)

Love, and you will have an occupation.
(Germany)

Nothing is so dead as yesterday's love.
(Austria)

X   Faithfulness is a sister of love.
(Belgium)

All shall be well, and Jack shall have his Jill.
(England)

The measure of our sacrifice is the measure of our love.
(Scotland)

✦ ✗ Immature love says: "I love you because I need you." Mature love says: "I need you because I love you."
(Confucianism)

✦ Singers of songs, lovers, and poets are privileged liars.
(Germany)

✦ Don't be so much in love that you can't tell when the rain is coming.
(Africa)

✗ ✦ He who loves without pleasure drinks without thirst, and eats without hunger.
(Norway)

Loving and singing are not to be forced.
(Greece)

Old love does not rust.
(Turkey)

When you have learned about love, you have learned about
the Great Spirit.
(Native American)

Inscribed on a bust of Cupid:
See here your master, be you who you may,
He is, or was, or shall be yours, one day.
(France)

Old love burns strong.
(United States)

Don't kiss and tell; honor in love is silence.
(Hebrew proverb)

Love has made heroes of many, and fools of many more.
(Sweden)

The head does not know how to play the part of the heart
for long.
(Poland)

Love laughs at caste distinctions.
(India)

Love locks no cupboards.
(England)

The feet of those we love make a bare path green.
(Italy)

To love and to be wise are two different things entirely.
(France)

Love is no impartial judge.
(Ireland)

Love, alms, devotion, and patience are the four elements
which make a layman a saint.
(Italy)

✗ Where there's no love, all of one's faults are apparent.
(Germany)

Love is the true price of love.
(Scotland)

Love is not merely saying; it is doing.
(Italy)

✗ Love knows no enemy.
(Japan)

To those in love miles are only paces.
(Germany)

Love is meat and drink and a blanket to boot. &
(United States)

Love is like dew that falls on both nettles and lilies. &
(Sweden)

Knowledge—know each other. Goodness—love each other.
(India)

&

A life without love is like a death without a witness.
(Holland)

If you love me let it appear. &
(Ireland)

Love is without law.
(England)

Happy's the wooing that's not long in doing.
(Scotland)

✗ As love thinks no evil, so envy speaks no good.
(Hungary)

The parentage of love is free; its parents are itself.
(Italy)

It is a happy chance if we continue to love a changed person.
(India)

The extreme form of passionate love is secret love.
(Japan)

Love sees only roses without thorns.
(Germany)

Love is the mother of love.
(England)

Where love is in the case, the doctor is an ass.
(United States)

Love is blind but sees afar.
(Italy)

When four eyes meet, then love comes into the heart.
(India)

Only love can overcome love.
(Germany)

Love makes a wit of the fool.
(England)

He who loves you will make you weep.
(Argentina)

Love and women prefer solitude.
(Italy)

No one should be allowed to die before he has loved.
(India)

The torch of love is lit in the kitchen.
(Poland)

In love it is the victim who looks most like a hero.
(Middle East)

Love and the gentle heart are but a single thing.
(Australia)

Such ever was love's way; to rise, it stoops.
(Lebanon)

It is sad not to be loved, but it is much sadder not
to be able to love.
(Finland)

Love is, above all, the gift of oneself to oneself.
(China)

When you love someone all your saved-up wishes
start coming true.
(Hebrew proverb)

What shall I do to love? Believe.
What shall I do to believe? Love.
(Ireland)

To fall in love is to create a religion that has a fallible god.
(Greece)

The richest love is that which submits to the arbitration
of time.
(Turkey)

Words are the weak support; love has no language
to be heard.
(Kenya)

Love is a mystery no man knows,
till it within his bosom glows.
(Ireland)

Love does not keep a ledger of the sins and failures of others.
(Italy)

Love is sharing a part of yourself with others.
(Jamaica)

This will be a better world when the power of love replaces the love of power.
(Ireland)

Love is a tyrant sparing none.
(Morocco)

Love lives on hope, and dies when hope is dead.
(Scotland)

✗ True love doesn't consist of holding hands, it consists of
holding hearts.
(Kenya)

With love, one can live even without happiness.
(Russia)

Love is a flame that sinks for lack of fuel.
(Sweden)

Loving someone is like taking vitamins for a healthy soul.
(Yiddish proverb)

Unable are the loved to die, for love is immortality.
(England)

   Without outward declarations, who can conclude an
inward love?
(Wales)

   Duty makes us do things well, but love makes us do them
beautifully.
(Korea)

   You can give without loving, but you can't love
without giving.
(Morocco)

   Love is more easily demonstrated than defined.
(Ancient Rome)

Love is the fairest flower that blooms in God's garden. ✘
(Lebanon)

Love is all we have; the only way that each can help the other.
(Jewish proverb)

Love begins with separateness and ends in oneness.
(Egypt)

Love is the irresistible desire to be desired irresistibly.
(Wales)

Love is the wisdom of the fool and the folly of the wise.
(United States)

When we are in love, we often doubt that which we
most believe.
(Afghanistan)

★ Love is an unusual game. There are either two winners
or none.
(Turkey)

Happiness is a healthy mental attitude, a grateful spirit, a
clean conscience, and a heart full of love.
(Scotland)

God Himself prays for the capacity to love.
(Russia)

It is love, not reason, that is stronger than death.
(Italy)

To be loved means to be consumed. To love is to give light with inexhaustible oil.
(Sudan)

Let the dead have the immortality of fame, the living the immortality of love.
(Turkey)

As selfishness clouds the mind, so love with its joy clears and sharpens the vision.
(United States)

Love is not love until love's vulnerable.
(England)

To love is to choose.
(Germany)

Love's gift cannot be given, it waits to be accepted.
(Poland)

One word frees us of all the weight and pain of life.
That word is love.
(Greece)

We don't love qualities, we love persons.
(Germany)

A very small degree of hope is sufficient to cause the birth of love.
(Holland)

The most lonely place in the world is the human heart when love is absent.
(Zanzibar)

X Love's reward comes in the knowing that an eye will sparkle upon our arrival.
(Ireland)

In love each strives to be the other, and both together make up one whole.
(Finland)

❧ A loveless life is a jeweled goblet that never contained
rare wine.
(Ancient Rome)

❧ Love is a crutch to be sure, but who among us has no need
for crutches?
(Ireland)

❧ Love consists in this: that two solitudes protect and border
and salute each other.
(Australia)

❧ Love is an act of endless forgiveness, a tender look that
becomes a habit.
(Norway)

✗ To ask advice on the rules of love is the same as asking advice on the rules of madness.

(France)

The great tragedy of life is not that men perish, but that they cease to love.

(England)

Better is a dinner of herbs where love is, than a stalled ox and hatred therewith.

(Proverbs 15:17)

The door to the human heart can be opened only from the inside.

(Spain)

To love without criticism is to be betrayed.
(Estonia)

The heart is happiest when it beats for others.
(United States)

It's so difficult to know what the people we love really need.
(Finland)

The only reason one loves is for his own pleasure.
(Denmark)

An old man loved is winter with flowers.
(Germany)

Oil, truth, and love always come to the top.
(Malagasy Republic)

Transplanted love seldom prospers.
(India)

Only love releases man from the fetters of nature.
(Germany)

Love is the meeting place between the human and divine.
(Belgium)

Love will always claim victory over the beautiful.
(Middle East)

Love without apprehension is the love that most deeply
touches the heart.
(Ireland)

✗ Love's highest reward is not what we get from it but what we
become through it.
(Poland)

What a mother sings to the cradle goes all the way down
to the coffin.
(Greece)

If wrinkles must be written upon our brows, let them not be
written upon the heart.
(United States)

✘ Mother is the name for God on the lips and in the hearts of little children.

(England)

Let your thoughts be over filled with love, and your love be ever filled with thought.

(Italy)

As the setting enhances a gem's charm, so also does love enhance life's charm.

(Africa)

Piety is the preeminent form of beauty, and its power lies in love, which is the gift of God.

(Hebrew proverb)

  x   We only see what we desire, only hear what we long for.

(Australia)

Love is the mother of wisdom.

(Spain)

Eat and drink below your means, clothe yourself according to your means, but love your wife and children beyond your means.

(Jewish proverb)

The thirst for love increases with every effort made to quench it.

(Wales)

Love alone dominates fear.
(United States)

A home without laughter is a home without love.
(Scotland)

Love is a privilege but it also has power.
(Austria)

Charm is more than beauty.
(Yiddish proverb)

O love, thy pains are worth more than all other pleasures.
(France)

  💕   Faith, love, and happiness are three elements that mysteriously blend together.

(Sweden)

  💕 ✗ To love and be loved are twin angels, each glorifying the other.

(Italy)

  💕   When you cannot love anymore, there is no longer a charm in living.

(Holland)

💕